God's

Mary Manz Simon
Illustrated by Carolyn Braun

Library of Congress cataloging in Publication Data

Simon, Mary Manz, 1948-
    God's children pray/Mary Manz Simon.
      p.   cm.
    Summary: A selection of traditional, familiar, and original
prayers for mealtime, morning and evening, and special days
such as birthdays, Christmas, and Thanksgiving.
    ISBN 0-570-04959-8
    1. Children—Prayer-books and devotions—English.
[1. Prayers. 2. Prayer books and devotions.] I. Title.
BV4870.S537   1989   89-7376
242'.82—dc20   AC

  6 7 8 9 10 11 12 13   06 05 04 03 02

In memory of my parents,
from whom I learned to pray.

Revelation 2:10

Acknowledgments

Morning Prayer 6; Mealtime Prayers 3, 9, 11; Bedtime Prayers 1, 8, 9; Special Times Prayer 6: from *Bible Stories For Me*, by Carol Greene. Copyright 1977 by Concordia Publishing House. Used by permission.

Morning Prayers 8; Mealtime Prayers 4, 13, 14, 15; Bedtime Prayers 4, 5, 6; Anytime Prayers 8, 9; Holiday Prayer 7: from *Prayers for the Very Young Child*, by Donald S. Roberts. Copyright 1981 by Concordia Publishing House. Used by permission.

Morning Prayers 10, 12; Mealtime Prayer 6; Bedtime Prayer 10: from *A Child's Garden of Prayer*, edited by H. W. Gockel and E. J. Saleska. Copyright 1948 by Concordia Publishing House. Used by permission.

Morning Prayer 11: from *Happy Times* vol. 16, no. 12 (September, 1980), edited by E. H. Gaulke. Copyright 1980 by Concordia Publishing House. Used by permission.

Morning Prayer 13; Mealtime Prayers 1, 2, 10; Bedtime Prayers 7, 11, 12; Anytime Prayer 10; Special Times Prayers 4, 12; Holiday Prayer 8: from *Little Folded Hands*, revised by Allan Jahsmann. Copyright 1959 by Concordia Publishing House. Used by permission.

Mealtime Prayer 5: from *Happy Times* vol. 17, no. 2 (November, 1980), edited by E. H. Gaulke. Copyright 1980 by Concordia Publishing House. Used by permission.

Anytime Prayer 6: from *Happy Times* vol. 23, no. 2 (November 1988), edited by E. H. Gaulke. Copyright 1988 by Concordia Publishing House. Used by permission.

Anytime Prayer 11: from *Happy Times* vol. 14, no 11 (August, 1978), Copyright 1978 by Concordia Publishing House. Used by permission.

Anytime Prayer 12: from *Bible Children I Know*, by Alice Stolper Peppler. Copyright 1971 by Concordia Publishing House. Used by permission.

Anytime Prayer 13: from *My Book of the Lord's Prayer*, by Eileen Lomasney. Copyright 1976 by Concordia Publishing House. Used by permission.

Holiday Prayer 11: from *Little Visits Every Day*, by Mary Manz Simon. Copyright 1988, 1995 by Concordia Publishing House. Used by permission.

Contents

Foreword

God's Children Pray is a beautiful way of stating an important fact: talking to God begins in early childhood.

In *God's Children Pray*, you will find brief, one-line prayers for the very young child. Then you will notice in each section that the prayers get longer, for this is a book that will grow up with children. The prayers in this slim volume will be learned easily and cherished for many years.

Morning, evening, and meals are the usual times for prayer. But the prayer life of a child can be nurtured anytime, on special days, and even on holidays. That's why you will find these prayer-starters, too.

May your life be richly blessed as God's children pray.

Morning Prayers

1

It's morning.
Thank You, Jesus. Amen.

2

Hooray, Hooray!
God made a new day. Amen.

3

Thank You, Jesus, for this day
To have the chance to learn and play.
Amen.

4

The sun is up, a new day's come.
I'll play and grow till this day's done.
Thank You, Jesus. Amen.

5

It's morning now, I lift my head
And sit up tall, jump out of bed.
Thank You, dear Jesus, for this day,
A time when I can learn and play. Amen.

6

Now the night has gone away.
Thank You, Lord, for this new day.
Stay with me the whole day through.
Help me to be good like You. Amen.

7

It's easiest to give You thanks
When day dawns bright and blue,
But I'm just glad to have the chance
To live this day for You.

Dear Jesus, help me try to act
And think and do and say
The way You'd like Your child to live
All through the coming day. Amen.

8

Dearest Jesus, lead the way
Through the coming hours of day.
Keep me safe in all I do,
Ever close, my Lord, to You. Amen.

9

Hi there, Jesus; it's a brand new day.
Be with me as I learn and play.
I don't know all that will go on,
But help me, Lord, know right
        from wrong. Amen.

10

Heavenly Father, hear my prayer;
Keep me in Thy loving care.
Guard me through the coming day,
In my work and in my play.
Keep me pure and strong and true;
Help me, Lord, Thy will to do. Amen.

11

Teach me to love;
Teach me to pray.
Jesus above,
Teach me Thy way.
Teach me how I,
In my small way,
Can, with Thy help,
Do good each day. Amen.

12

In the early morning,
With the sun's first rays,
All God's little children
Thank, and pray, and praise.

Always in Thy keeping,
Jesus, Savior dear,
Whether waking, sleeping,
Be Thou ever near. Amen.

13

I thank You, Jesus, for the night
And for the pleasant morning light,
For rest and food and loving care
And all that makes the world so fair.

Help me to do the things I should,
To be to others kind and good,
In all I do at work or play,
To grow more loving every day. Amen.

Mealtime Prayers

1

Thank You, Jesus, for this food. Amen.

2

Come, Lord Jesus, be our Guest,
And let Your gifts to us be blessed.
Amen.

3

God is great, God is good;
And we thank Him for our food. Amen.

4

Bless this food,
Dear Lord, we pray.
Make us thankful every day. Amen.

5

For warm, safe homes,
　　for clothes to wear,
For food to eat and food to share—
Thank You, Jesus. Amen.

6

Our hands we fold,
Our heads we bow;
For food and drink
We thank Thee now. Amen.

7

For health and strength
And daily food,
We praise Your name,
O Lord. Amen.

8

Dear Jesus, now I bow my head
Before I eat this daily bread.
To You, O Lord, my thanks I say,
For food and drink another day. Amen.

Feb.

9

Dear Lord, hear us pray.
Bless our food today.
Lord, we pray again:
Bless us, too. Amen.

10

Oh, give thanks unto the Lord,
For He is good;
For His mercy endures forever. Amen.

March

11

Thank You for the world so sweet.
Thank You for the food we eat.
Thank You for the birds that sing.
Thank You, God, for everything. Amen.

12

We thank You, Lord, for happy hearts,
For sun and rainy weather.
We thank You for the food we eat
And that we are together. Amen.

13

Father, make me thankful
For food that may not be
The food I think is best to eat,
But still is good for me. Amen.

April

14

Heavenly Father, let me see
All the ways that You bless me.
Thank You for the food I'm fed;
Thank You for my daily bread. Amen.

May

15

Now we bow our heads to pray;
Thank You for this food today.
Now we fold our hands and say,
Thank You, Lord, in every way. Amen.

16

Sometimes, I guess, it's hard to say,
"Dear Jesus, thanks for food today."
Help me be grateful, for I'm blessed,
Dear Jesus, as Your dinner guest. Amen.

17

I thank You, Jesus, for this food.
I'm sure it will do lots of good
To fill me up with energy
And live this day, O Lord, for Thee.
Amen.

Bedtime Prayers

1

Bless everyone I love, God.
And bless me, too. Amen.

2

Bless me as I fall asleep.
Send Your angels watch to keep. Amen.

3

It's time for me to go to sleep.
Dear Jesus, now I pray:
Thank You, dear Lord, for all I've done.
I thank You for today. Amen.

4

Gentle Jesus, hear my prayer.
Keep me safe this night.
Stay with me until the dark
Becomes the morning light. Amen.

5

Lord Jesus, keep me in Thy sight
Through the coming hours of night.
Then when morning sunlight beams
Wake me, Lord, from sleepy dreams.
Amen.

6

Dearest Lord, I come to Thee;
Please hear me as I pray.
Keep me safe all through the night
And bring a bright new day. Amen.

7

Now I lay me down to sleep;
I pray Thee, Lord, Thy child to keep.
When in the morning I awake,
Help me the path of love to take,
And this I ask for Jesus' sake. Amen.

8

Now I lay me down to sleep.
I pray You, Lord, Your child to keep.
Send happy dreams and near me stay
Until another happy day. Amen.

9

Jesus, tender Shepherd, hear me.
Bless Your little child tonight.
Through the darkness,
        please be near me.
Keep me safe till morning's light. Amen.

10

Dear Father, whom I cannot see,
Smile down from heaven on little me.

Let angels through the darkness spread
Their holy wings about my bed.

And keep me safe, because I am
The heavenly Shepherd's little lamb.
Amen.

11

The day is done;
O God the Son,
Look down upon
Thy little one!

O God of Light,
Keep me this night,
And send to me
Thy angels bright.

I need not fear
If Thou art near;
Thou art my Savior,
Kind and dear. Amen.

12

Now the light has gone away;
Savior, listen while I pray,
Asking Thee to watch and keep
And to send me quiet sleep.

Jesus, Savior, wash away
All that has been wrong today;
Help me every day to be
Good and gentle, more like Thee.

Let my near and dear ones be
Always near and dear to Thee.
Oh, bring me and all I love
To Thy happy home above. Amen.

Anytime Prayers

1

It's today.
Thanks, Jesus. Amen.

2

Dear Jesus,
I love You. Amen.

3

Jesus my Savior, kind and true,
Jesus my Savior, I love You. Amen.

4

I'm Your child, for You love me.
You died and rose so I could be
All full of hope and joy and love
Which come from You, my Lord, above.
Amen.

5

Be near me, Lord Jesus;
    I ask Thee to stay
Close by me forever and love me, I pray.
Bless all the dear children
    in Thy tender care.
And take us to heaven to live with Thee
        there. Amen.

6

Thank You, God, for friends at play.
Thank You for each brand new day.
Thank You for the morning light.
Thank You for our beds at night. Amen.

7

Praise God, from whom all blessings flow;
Praise Him, all creatures here below;
Praise Him above, O heavenly host;
Praise Father, Son, and Holy Ghost.
Amen.

8

I am Your child, O dearest Lord.
Each day I pray to Thee.
Help me to love all people
The way that You love me. Amen.

9

Bless me, dearest Lord; I pray
That I may bless someone today.
Show me how to share Your joy
With every girl and every boy. Amen.

10

Jesus, Friend of little children,
Be a Friend to me;
Take my hand and ever keep me
Close to Thee. Amen.

11

O Jesus, so kind; O Jesus, so mild;
You care for me, a little child.
Your love surrounds me day to day;
You bend and listen when I pray.
O Jesus, so kind; O Jesus, so mild.

O Jesus, so kind; O Jesus so mild;
Be always near Your little child.
Protect all other children, too,
And help us grow to be like You.
O Jesus, so kind; O Jesus, so mild.

12

God, be in our heads
 And in our understanding.
God, be in our eyes
 And in our looking.
God, be in our mouths
 And in our speaking.
God, be in our hearts
 And in our loving.
God, be in our bodies
 And in our doing.
God, be in us; Be in us always.
 In Jesus' name, Amen.

13

One day a friend asked Jesus
To teach us how to pray,
And Jesus did—then gave us all
A perfect prayer to say.

Our Father in heaven,
hallowed be Your name,
Your kingdom come,
Your will be done
on earth as in heaven.
Give us today our daily bread.
Forgive us our sins
as we forgive those
who sin against us.
Lead us not into temptation,
but deliver us from evil.
For the kingdom, the power,
and the glory are Yours
now and forever. Amen.

Special Times Prayers

Naptime

1

It's time to nap, I'd rather play;
The day's just partly done.
Be with me now, dear Jesus,
And I'll wake to have more fun! Amen.

Birthday

2

Dear Jesus, now my thanks I say
For giving me this nice birthday. Amen.

3

My birthday came, it really did!
My birthday is today.
Help me to use this special time
To thank You, Lord, I pray. Amen.

4

We thank the Lord who kept you
All through the passing year;
He put His arms around you
And gave you health and cheer.

Now we will pray together
That He will keep you still
And make the next year happy
And help you do His will. Amen.

Sickness

5

I'm sick today;
Help me, I pray. Amen.

6

Tender Jesus, meek and mild,
Look on me, a little child.
Help me, if it is Your will,
To recover from all ill. Amen.

7

I don't feel good; this is no fun.
Why am I sick today?
Dear Jesus, help me know You're here;
With me You'll always stay. Amen.

Growing Up

8

It's not so easy growing up
When things don't go my way.
Remind me patience and a smile
Will brighten up my day.

But even when I make mistakes,
I know You'll always be
My Jesus, my forgiving Lord,
Because You do love me. Amen.

9

Sometimes I sit and worry
When I've done something bad.
I hide my tears and try to smile,
But worries make me sad.

Help me remember, Jesus,
That You will care for me
Through loving people, angels, too.
With me You'll always be.

New Baby

10

Dear Jesus,
You gave me a new baby,
All little, noisy, warm.
Be with my little baby,
And keep us both from harm.

I know You love this baby.
I know You love me, too.
Help me to act as a child of Yours
In what I say and do. Amen.

Church and School

11

Father, bless our school today;
Be in all we do or say;
Be in ev'ry song we sing;
Ev'ry prayer to Thee we bring. Amen.

12

Dear Jesus, bless each little child
And keep us all, we pray,
Safe in Your loving care until
Another holy day. Amen.

Holiday Prayers

Valentine's Day

1

A day of hearts,
A day of love,
Sent to us
From You above.
Thanks, Jesus. Amen.

2

The cards all say that "I love you"
With pink and purple hearts, it's true.
But I don't need a valentine,
To know that You, my Lord, are mine.
Amen.

Easter

3

It's Easter Day
And I can say,
"Thank You, Jesus, for today!" Amen.

4

The rabbits hop, the chicks say "peep,"
And spring is on the way.
But You, dear Lord, rose from the dead
To make this Easter Day.
Thank You, Jesus. Amen.

5

Dear Jesus,

    I'm working hard to learn about
What happened Easter Day,
    When Mary went to the garden tomb
And heard the angel say:

    "He is not here. He's risen!
Now tell to one and all."
    And Mary ran right down the road.
"He's risen!" they heard her call.

    Help me to learn and understand
What Easter's all about
    So, when the people greet today,
I too can sing and shout:
    Alleluia!
Thank You, Jesus. Amen.

Thanksgiving

6

It doesn't seem like a holiday,
I don't get anything new.
But all year long the love I get
Comes because of You. Amen.

7

Teach me to be thankful, Lord,
In everything I do;
For all the things I call my own
Are really gifts from You. Amen.

8

God made the sun,
And God made the tree;
God made the mountains,
And God made me.

I thank You, O God,
For the sun and the tree,
For making the mountains
And for making me. Amen.

Christmas

9

There's one thing I would like to say,
"I'm glad that Jesus came today." Amen.

10

"It's Christmas! It's Christmas!"
I sing and shout.
Your birthday, Your birthday,
Is what it's about.
Happy birthday, Jesus! Amen.

The signs of Christmas are around
In stores and malls, cities, towns.
Help me remember as I pray,
What really counts on Christmas Day
Is You are born, Christ Jesus, Lord.
Your love, God's love, is what is heard.
The wreaths and stars all shining bright
Are just for You on Christmas night.
Amen.